DATA LAKE

AWS & AZURE
DATA LAKE, BIG DATA Solutions & Security
(Introduction)

By

Suresh Nair
Poornima Suresh

TRADEMARK ACKNOWLEDGMENTS

I dedicate this book to my mother, B. Santhamma, whose life served as an inspiration and motivation to me and all those around her. Her love and affection will always be remembered and cherished.

This book is also dedicated to my father, Chandrasekharan Nair, as well as my siblings Sujatha, Sushama & Subhash whose support and guidance continues to have an immeasurable impact in my life.

-- Suresh

I dedicate this book to my Grandmother, B. Santhamma, whose love and affection will always be remembered and cherished.

-- Poornima

CREDITS

Graphic Illustrators:

      Poornima Suresh

Cover designers:

      Poornima Suresh

Proofreaders:

      Poornima Suresh

Reviewers:

      Bhuvanraj Deepak

      Steve Smith

Critics:

      Resmi Suresh

Research Associates:

      Poornima Suresh

Authors:

      Suresh Nair

      Poornima Suresh

CREDITS

I acknowledge my classmates from three decades ago Venu for all the technical discussions and tips, John P Joseph for always inspiring me with all his innovative ideas and everything he shared with me, Sethu for the wonderful friendship, Santhosh for all blessings shared, Jose, Paulson, Eldho, Manoj, Biji, Unni, Sabu for all the lighter moments we shared after the college when our paths converged again at different points in life. Jini, Sreedevi, Prasanna, Seethamma and all our classmates whose fond memories still linger in my mind have helped & inspired me to get where I am today.

I express my deep gratitude to Murali Peddakotla & Sunitha for their immeasurable support extended to me & my family and have touched my life in many inconceivable ways. I thank the families of Hari & Jayanthi Sreeraj, Monai's family , Jeminis & Roopa who also have impacted my life deeply.

Ajitkumar L, Vivekanandan, Moosad Uncle and their families bestowed affection friendship, and support which helped me sail through the thick and thin of my life and will remain very dear to the depths of heart.

The love, care and affection of my uncles and aunties from my patriarchal Valloor family (Sarasamma,Vasudevan,Santhamma, Ponnamma, Ramachandran, Balachandran, Radhamani) and those from my Matriarchal Mavilatharayil family (Somasekharan, Sumathi(Umbotti), Prema(Sridevi) & Sreekumar) gave me the strength to walk every step of my life. Haritattan, Rajesh, Sreekumar chettan, Anil, Sreemol, Abhi, Vaavi, Lekha, Leena, Rama, Praseetha, Prasad,Ajith,Usha, Unni, Bindu, Sathichetchi, Prasanna chectchi,

Sweet memories of the stories from my Grandparents (Govindan Nair, Kesavan Nair, Narayani Amma, Krishnan Nair, & Bhavani Amma that imparted me the belief in Lord Krishna, Lord Rama, Lord Ganesha, Godess Lakshmi & Godess Saraswathi, Sri Swami Ayyappan & Malikapurathu Bhagavathi instilled faith and courage I needed every time in my journey this far.

My siblings Sujatha, Sushama & Subash have been of immense support in my life along with Resmi, Mini, Satheesh & Ramdas. We share a lot of fond memories with Unnikuttan, Kunju, Poornima, Bhavani, Radha, Vishnu & Krishnakaanth. Jose Uncle, Shirley Aunty, Ravi Uncle, Aunty, Ganesh, Sunil & Sreekumar Chetan along with their families have a special place in my life next to my own family. A few of my acquaintances I would like to acknowledge for having made a considerable attachment to me are Sanjay, Madhu, Thomas, Dileep, and Santhosh Pillai. Bhal, & Rohit, Ernie, Chris, Steve & Janet are greatly appreciated and acknowledged for mentoring, and shaping my career & Life. Having seen them writing books Dr.A.K.B Pillai & Dona have been a source of inspiration for me in my writing endeavors.

5

TABLE OF CONTENTS

DATA LAKES: AWS & AZURE Data Lake, Big Data Solutions & Security (Introduction), is the first of a series of books to be published on Big data Infrastructure Cloud Platform security. This book is intended to provide a very basic guidance for securing the AWS cloud offerings from Amazon Inc. and Azure cloud offering on Data Lakes. This book may be used by the end clients and IT professionals while planning and setting up a secure cloud infrastructure or while carrying out infrastructure migrations to AWS or Azure cloud.

The intention of the authors is to present a document in an organized structure around the concept of Data Lakes and information on many of the security tools & features in the big data echo system. An effort is made to introduce important concepts, features and services offered by Amazon Inc. and Microsoft Inc., and provide a point of reference to the reader, enabling them do the deep dive as needed on specific domains of their interest in order to secure their infrastructural assets.

The authors hope that this book will help the end users and IT professionals in setting up a **secure Data Lake infrastructure** by providing a single platform of reference where they can get familiarized with the basic concepts and the security features of AWS & Azure cloud offering relevant to Data Lake technology and from there they can do further deep dive into their domains of interest in securing their AWS/Azure cloud infrastructure.

An earnest effort is made to extend credit to all the references used in the preparation of this document under the **credits** and any omission there is not intentional and shall be corrected upon intimation.

DATA LAKE

Definition of Data Lake

A data lake can be defined as data store or repository of huge amounts of analytically useful data. The data is stored, in general, in its native or raw format. The data is stored in a flat architecture rather than in a hierarchical way like data warehouse stores in which case data is in files or folders. A unique identifier is assigned to the data elements in a data lake and may be also tagged with a set of extended metatags. "Schema-on-read" approach is employed while running analytics. Any BI request is processed by querying this large Data Lake, with no specific schema or data requirements, for relevant data elements and the resulting smaller dataset is analyzed to generate the final result. In many situations data mining and business analytics tools are applied to the raw data that is stored in typically a Hadoop object storage.

The data stored in Data Lake can be of any type, structured data (schema with rows and columns defined), semi structured data (CSV, XML, JSON, log files etc.) and unstructured data (PDFs, Documents, media files and emails).

Organization may choose to have multiple data lakes to manage security compliances requirements, data protection, availability requirements, Disaster recovery and Business Continuance.

Data lake can also be made data-aware and storage -aware by tagging and by adding metadata.

The raw data may also be automatically transformed before capturing to the data lake, a process called data refining (IBM).

Data ingest can be derived from in house databases or data warehouse repositories.

Data Lakes can be used to create large collections of structured, semi-structured or unstructured data generated by multiple sources.

Apache Hadoop based Data Lakes are being used to store data for profiling, predictive analysis, data discovery, Machine learning, visualization etc.

A Data lake that provides a very little value to the users or one that is inaccessible to the users or one that is in a deteriorated state is called a Data Swamp.

Data Lake is a store of raw data (low data quality) which can be structured, semi structured or non-structured with a schema-on-read approach for use by data scientists and analysts for profiling, predictive analysis, data discovery, Machine learning, visualization etc. Data loaded as from the source nearly untransformed state. The data lake ingest almost all the data and not normally transformed prior to loading, transformation. The data transformation is done at the stage when data is read for reporting (schema-on-read). Data Lake supports all data type and all data formats regardless of its source and structure.

Data warehouse stores curated (cleaned, enriched or transformed) data (current and historic) extracted from OLTP systems with a schema-on-write approach for use by business analysts for operational reporting purposes in general. Its data structure is designed to meet specific business reporting needs. Data warehouse supports specific intended data types and structures.

The data ware use is intended for use by a small set of users, BAs who would like to generate and see specific reports. Data lake is can accommodate a wider spectrum of users like data scientists, BAs and other users who might want to generate reports that be based on the historic data for which a ware house was not designed or implemented.

Data warehouse technology has matured over a period of time in terms data security. Since the data is stored based on a predefined schema, better security controls can be implemented. But Data Lake is a nascent technology and since it does not confirm to a specific schema, the implementation of data security of data lakes is yet to mature.

Data Lake based on Hadoop is cheaper since it is open source technology relying on commodity hardware, but data warehousing software are often commercial software running on high end servers and involves licensing fee.

Data Lake ingest all types of data and the data scientists and developers can dynamically design and redesign their models on the fly without any change to the data structures. Data warehouse structural changes could get time consuming depending on the size of the database and its dependency on the business process for data ingest.

Data warehouse is implements the Extract, Transform and Load (ETL) methodology, where Data lake implements Extract, Load and Transform (ELT) approach.

DATAMART

DataMart is a store of cleansed, curated data for easy consumption. It can be considered smaller subset of data warehouse (James Dixon: Pentaho)

DATABRICKS

Azure Databricks is an Apache Spark based analytics platform integrates with Azure IoT Hub, Azure Data Lake Store, Azure SQL Data Warehouse, Azure Cosmos DB, Azure Blob storage, Azure Event Hubs for data source.

This fully managed cloud-native platform includes a set of analytics technologies like SQL, Streaming, MLlib, and GraphX. As a Mocrosoft cloud offering, Databricks natively integrates with other Azure services such as Power BI, SQL Data Warehouse, and Cosmos DB and enterprise-grade Azure security (Active Directory integration, compliance etc.).

Azure Databricks is certified by HIPAA, SOC2-Type2, ISO27001 and ISO27018.

(Extracted from https://azure.microsoft.com/en-us/services/databricks/ 5.00am, on 08/09/2018)

Data ware house typically address specific needs of operational reporting of an organization and holds curated (cleaned, transformed & structured) data and the data and data structure are normally optimized for that business purpose. And it is meant to be used by specific user groups (BAs) and optimized for that purpose. So that does not have to be replaced unless the data lake can be used as effectively as the data warehouse for the same purpose.

Data Lake is not designed or optimized for any specific business purpose and holds all or most of the data in its nearly native, raw form & structure and is created with a schema-on-read approach where the schema is defined while reading the data from the data lake at the time analysis. The data lake can serve a wide spectrum of users (data scientists, BAs and any other intended user authorized to use the data). The data lakes are mostly used by data scientists and analysts for profiling, predictive analysis, data discovery, Machine learning, visualization etc. Setting up the data lake for such purposes is more efficient than creating individual data warehouse solution for each and every one of such requirement.

In certain cases if the data lake can efficiently and effectively generate the intended Operational reports for which a data warehouse solution exists, a phased approach to discontinue the data ware house may be adopted.

In most cases since the intended audience or users are different both can co-exist serving different target groups and purposes. This Hybrid model is quite often the appropriate one.

x

TYPICAL SOURCES OF BIG DATA

- *IOT sensor data*
- *GPS trails*
- *Website clickstream data*
- *Social media*
- *Emails*
- *Server logs*
- *Mobile device apps*
- *Existing data warehouse databases*
- *Enterprise wide application data*
- *Public records data*
- *Commercial transaction data*
- *Data archives of all types.*
- *Media (audio, video)*
- *Business application data*

1. Central Repository: *Typically a Data Lake Serves as a central repository of all analytically meaningful, raw data with index of the inventory of data and its metadata (source, version, veracity, data quality).The data lake allows the user to catalogue and index the data. A data lake should have a defined mechanisms to collect, store, and catalog, secure, analyze data, aid collaboration & sharing of the discoveries.*

2. Secure access of data: *Proper access, authentication, authorization and auditing techniques.*

3. Data quality: *Is one of the major challenges in data lake implementations. If designed to ingest data without compromising the data format, it would provide data scientists with greater flexibility to discover meaningful information. Sarbanes-Oxley, Dodd-Frank, Basel III and Solvency II are some of the existing laws and standards and demands a high level of accuracy on the corporate reports that are submitted which in turn implies high quality of data from which those reports are generated.*

4. Storage quality: *Considering the amount, velocity, veracity of data ingest and the*

analytical processing that are being performed on the data, it is imperative that the data lake storage infrastructure is robust enough to handle the current load and anticipated future loads.

5. Scalability: *The data intake into the repository is expected to grow exponentially in the Data Lake / big data domain so any implementation architecture should be highly scalable to accommodate that growth.*

6. Ensure data protection and availability: *Meet the operational DR and BI requirements*

7. Ensure IT governance: *enforce rules and policies on quality and quantity of the data coming in and out of the data lake, retention policies of the data etc. Data security policies to protect the data-in-transit and data-at-rest from internal/external threats by implementing secure authentication, authorization and encryption policies and practices.*

8. Analytic Technology Agnostic: *Provide analytics to various analytical tools (Hadoop, data workflows etc.) to enable critical decision making.*

9. Analytic query performance: *Considering the fact that the data lake comprise of huge amounts of structured/semi structured/unstructured data, the performance of the query ran on the data depends largely on the selecting the infrastructure.*

10. Agility of the data source: *should enable multiple analytical tools perform analysis in shared data-mining environment. It provides an agility over traditional data warehouses which typically old transformed data.*

11. Technology agnostic: *The data lake architecture should be analytics technology agnostic to the extent possible. There are many vendor specific analytic tools (Apache Hadoop, Apache Spark, Presto and many BI tools)*

Evaluate the expected business outcome:

Identify the business requirements and evaluate the achievability of it by implementing the data lake.

Team building (with Skilled Talent):

An ideal data lake would need a pool of highly skilled Talents.

Data scientists: with the domain knowledge of the business to work in close association with business

Data engineers: to design and architect the data lake in close association with the data scientist and to maintain and administer the data lake.

Software engineers: to integrate different software tools to generate the intelligence out of the data lake in c lose association with data scientists and business.

Data source Integration:

Existing BI platforms: Identify the existing Business Intelligence platforms, tools and the dashboard. Identify the sources for pulling the data, like the data from existing internal IT infrastructure, External data sources etc.

Mode of data ingest: Evaluate how the data s going to be ingested into the data lake. a) Raw data is directly ingested or b) does it need an initial cataloguing or indexing of the raw data to transform it.

Data analysis platforms: Is the data from the data lake is going out to a structured (oracle DB, MySQL DB or SQL server DB) or unstructured analytical platform (Hadoop)

Implement a data lake that can be integrated for data ingestion from the existing data sources with due consideration of adaptation to emerging, futuristic technologies.

Data preparation:

Irrespective of whether the platform is Data Lake or a traditional relational database data handing is easy and data quality is better if the ingested is prepared for the relevant data handling

Data governance:

Data governance is essential to a successful data lake implementation to ensure Data quality and data security. Too much of governance can impact the efficiency and agility of the discovery process but too less of governance can cause data compromise and legal implication to the organization. Implement a good a data governance practices, processes and policies.

Capital layout on infrastructure Investment:

Consider investing in the in-house IT infrastructure or investing in cloud solutions. Setting up In-house infrastructure may involve costly hardware, expensive software tools and licensing expenses for it. Cloud solutions can be started off with low monthly or annual expenses and tools that are freely and readily available from cloud service providers, but it can turn out to be more expensive as the data lake grows in size. Cloud solutions offer better security, quick deployment, better availability, scalability, very high elasticity, frequent system/feature/functionality updates from most vendors, wide/global geographic coverage, and costs proportional to actual utilization.

Amazon AWS offers the data lake solution and the following is an extract from microsoft.com extracted on 08/07/2018 at 9.20 am US EST from the link https://aws.amazon.com/big-data/datalakes-and-analytics/what-is-a-data-lake/

"Build your Data Lakes in the cloud on AWS

AWS provides the most secure, scalable, comprehensive, and cost-effective portfolio of services that enable customers to build their data lake in the cloud, analyze all their data, including data from IoT devices with a variety of analytical approaches including machine learning."

Amazon AWS offers reliable, secure, and scalable object storage Amazon Simple Storage Service (S3) and low-cost, long-term archiving and backup solution Amazon Glacier.

Microsoft Inc. Azure offers the data lake solution and the following is an extract from microsoft.com extracted on 08/07/2018 at 9.09 am US EST from the link https://azure.microsoft.com/en-us/solutions/data-lake/

"Azure Data Lake includes all the capabilities required to make it easy for developers, data scientists, and analysts to store data of any size, shape, and speed, and do all types of processing and analytics across platforms and languages. It removes the complexities of ingesting and storing all of your data while making it faster to get up and running with batch, streaming, and interactive analytics. Azure Data Lake works with existing IT investments for identity, management, and security for simplified data management and governance. It also integrates seamlessly with operational stores and data warehouses so you can extend current data applications."

By virtue of the fact that the Hadoop is collection of projects, subprojects and vendor extensions, managing security of the platform is a challenge at an integrated platform level. Proper access, authentication, authorization, encryption data masking of data (in motion as well as at rest), auditing techniques and Disaster Recovery & Backup should be considered to secure sensitive data.

Authentication – verify the identity of the user/service/app is legitimate

Authorization – the function of managing (allowing or denying) of the privilege levels of users to access and act on data or resources (file permissions, ACL).

To allow users different levels of access to the same data sets, data masking capabilities (Dataguise) should be implemented. Authentication tools should be used to manage user credentials and role credentials at the user/application level. Some of the tools available from Hadoop echo system are as well as some vendor products are listed below.

Microsoft AD: Active Directory Services from Microsoft manages users, groups and services. Authorized users gain access to Hadoop services defined in AD Kerberos via AD groups.

MIT Kerberos & SPNEGO: *Used in Linux/Unix based systems Authenticated users use "tickets" to access the services. SPNEGO extends Kerberos authentication to web application and portals.*

LDAP Open LDAP: *Used in Linux/Unix based systems.*

Apache Knox – *An API gateway that serves as a single point of access for all REST API communication with Hadoop clusters.*

Apache Sentry - *module that provides role based authorization of users/apps to data and metadata in HDFS via RBAC, for Hadoop services, led by Cloudera.*

Apache Ranger - *for administering security policies across Hadoop echo system and Key management service. Led by Hortonworks.*

Rhino - *Encryption and key management. Authorization framework across Hadoop projects and sub projects. Led by Intel.*

Apache Falcon - *A data governance engine that can be used to define and schedule data management and governance policies across the Hadoop environment.*

Cloudera Navigator Encrypt: *A scalable, AES-256 encryption solution to secure Hadoop filesystem data*

Cloudera Navigator key trustee Server:

HDFS: *TDE, Hive CLE, Hbase. Encryptions native for data at rest. Open source eCryptfs (file level), LUKS, DMCrypt (volume level) encryption.*

SSL & SASL: *AES-256 for SSL & DTP with SASL for data in motion.*

Dataguise - *used to automatically mask personally identifiable information (PII) from both Hadoop and NoSQL databases.*

Cloudera Manager, Apache Ambari & MapR control system: *These Common management User Interfaces allow examination of log files of different Hadoop components via the central interface.*

Cloudera Navigator Audit, Apache Atlas: *Capture data lineage, filesystem, and database and authorization component changes and provide interfaces to conduct audit queries.*

Hbase, Kafka: *Near real time mirroring of data*

MapR-FS & HDFS: *The distributed filesystems, using scheduled file copy mechanism, can replicate to another remote cluster.*

Apache Hive metastore: *records audit trail of Hive interaction.*

Any entity who does business in the European Union (EU) or collect data on EU citizens, shall demonstrate compliance with the General Data Protection Regulation (GDPR):

- *Identify all of the privacy data, where it is stored, who has permission to access it, who has permission to manipulate it, who works on it, and how the end-user privacy is protected.*
- *Adopt new governance procedures.*
- *Create position for data controllers (define and ensure compliance).*
- *Create position for processors (maintain & process data).*
- *Create position for protection officers (oversee GDDPR compliance and data security strategy).*

Review the following for GDPR compliance and ensure that the evaluation criteria are met.

- *Data storage and containment,*
- *Encryption of data in store and in motion,*
- *Cognitive analytics,*
- *Common cloud based infrastructure,*
- *Regional regulations.*

Implement the Unified endpoint management (UEM) the modern approach to mobile device management (MDM) and enterprise mobility management (EMM), provides a centralized view of all the devices, users, apps, and data to help the enterprise to track its ongoing compliance goals. The UEM solution, IBM MaaS360 with Watson meets the requirements an enterprises to both demonstrate and help maintain compliance with GDPR. MaaS360 offers the full sets of features and functions to enable an organization meet compliance requirements, like GDPR and beyond, and are specific to your country, region, or industry. Visit IBM.com/MaaS360 for more information.

☒

STANDARDS, PRACTICES, CERTFICATIONS

SOC   -Service Organization Control
FISMA   -Federal Information Security Management Act
DoD   - Department of Defense
DIACAP   -Department of Defense Information Assurance Certification and
Accreditation Process
FEDRAM   -Federal Risk and Authorization Management Program
DOD SRG   -DoD Cloud Computing Security Requirements Guide
CJIS   - Criminal Justice Information Services
NIST   -National Institute of Standards and Technology
PCIDSS   -Payment Card Industry Data Security Standard level1
ISO   -International Organization for Standardization ISO9001/ISO
270001
USITAR   -US International Traffic in Arms Regulations
VPAT   -Voluntary Product Accessibility Template Section 508
FIPS   -Federal Information Processing Standard 140-2
HIPPA   -Health Insurance Portability and Accountability Act
HITECH   - Health Information Technology for Economic and Clinical Health
Act
FERPA   - Family Educational Rights and Privacy Act
CSA   - Cloud Security Alliance
MPAA   -Motion Picture Association of America.
NIAP   - National Information Assurance Partnership
NISPOM   - National Industrial Security Program Operating Manual
OSPP   - Operating System Protection Profile
CAPP   - Controlled Access Protection Profile
EAL   - Evaluation Assurance Level
STIG   - Security Technical Implementation Guides
SOX   - Sarbanes Oxley Act
COBIT   - Control Objectives for Information and related Technology.

REFERENCES

https://searchaws.techtarget.com/definition/data-lake

*https://searchcio.techtarget.com/news/2240240456/Hadoop
-security-Dont-build-your-data-lake-without-it*

*https://searchcio.techtarget.com/news/2240240456/Hadoop
-security-Dont-build-your-data-lake-without-it*

*https://searchmobilecomputing.techtarget.com/UEM/Meetin
g-GDPR-Compliance-with-Endpoints-and-Mobile-
Devices?asrc=SS_scio_SN-2240240456*

*https://aws.amazon.com/big-data/datalakes-and-
analytics/*

Suresh Nair. B.Tech, PGDCA, MAS

Suresh is an IT professional with over 25 years of experience as a consultant with fortune 50 institutions in airline, financial, insurance, pharmaceutical, domains & government agencies performing data center migration, application/database migration and server migrations from physical to physical environment and physical to virtual environment involving Sun Solaris, IBM AIX, VMware ESX and AWS (Amazon Cloud Services).

Suresh is experienced in Information Security baselines, Standards, Best practices for OS hardening, Compliance requirements, Vulnerability Scanning & penetration testing, Monitoring, Log analysis & Intrusion detection systems. As an Architect of data centers / networks / systems (on premise and AWS cloud) he has extensive experience in UNIX server/Web/Intranet Security plans and procedures based on server hardening (Solaris, AIX & Red Hat Linux) and access/asset/scanning/monitoring/logging policies and procedures.

He has been involved in setting up and managing heterogeneous LAN environments in capacities as an administrator, AWS Cloud administrator and Information Technology Security Consultant and Architect. He is also experienced in Database Administration (Oracle, MySQL) & Performance Tuning.

Other projects he has been involved with include, architecting & configuring High Availability Clustering (HACMP) AIX clusters, VERITAS Cluster based Solaris clusters(SAP), RHEL clusters, Secure JBOSS Application server load balanced clusters, Web logic Application clusters, Oracle RAC, MySQL replications, and installation of Hadoop clusters.

Backup/Disaster recovery systems project functions he has been performing involved: Evaluate, plan, architect, document and execute disaster recovery and business continuance (DR/BC) plans and procedures for airline / financial / insurance / pharmaceutical / government domains involving cluster / SAN Storage (SUN, EMC, Hitachi, Dell, and Alexandria) subsystems, backup, virtualization (AWS, VMware, SUN (LDOM, Zone), IBM (LPAR)) based solutions for SLAs of varying RPOs & RTOs.

Poornima Suresh. BE, ME

Poornima holds a Master's degree in computer engineering at Rutgers University. She completed her Bachelor's degree in electrical and computer engineering from the Honors College at Rutgers. While at Rutgers, she was a member of the IEEE Robotics Club, and participated in published academic research.

Her interests include robotics, machine learning, cloud computing, and cybersecurity. She volunteers at a clinic and develops mobile apps for medical diagnostics in her spare time.

OTHER BOOKS BY THE AUTHORS

AWS cloud Security Best Practices   : Suresh Nair

BITCOIN (Mining, Storing and Trading): Suresh Nair & Poornima Suresh

FEEDBACK

Please send us your feedback to emailsureshnair@gmail.com